SUMMARY
of Alan Alda's
IF I UNDERSTOOD YOU, WOULD I HAVE THIS LOOK ON MY FACE?

My Adventures into the Art and Science of Relating and Communicating

by SUMOREADS

Copyright © 2017 by SUMOREADS. All rights reserved. This book or parts thereof may not be reproduced in any form, stored in any retrieval system, or transmitted in any form by any means—electronic, mechanical, photocopy, recording, or otherwise—without prior written permission of the publisher, except as provided by United States of America copyright law. This is an unofficial summary and is not intended as a substitute or replacement for the original book.

TABLE OF CONTENTS

EXECUTIVE SUMMARY 6

PART I: RELATING IS EVERYTHING 8

Chapter 1: Relating, It's the Cake 8
Chapter 2: Theatre Games with Engineers 8
Chapter 3: The Heart and Head of Communication 9
Chapter 4: The Mirror Exercise 9
Chapter 5: Observation Games 10
Chapter 6: Making it Clear and Vivid 10
Chapter 7: Reading Minds Helen Reiss and Matt Lerner 11
Chapter 8: Teams 11
Chapter 9: Total Listening Starts with Where They Are 12
Chapter 10: Listening from the Board Room to the Bedroom 12
Chapter 11: Training Doctors to Have More Empathy .. 13

PART II: GETTING BETTER AT READING OTHERS 14

Chapter 12: My Life as a Lab Rat 14
Chapter 13: Working Alone on Building Empathy 14
Chapter 14: Dark Empathy 15
Chapter 15: Reading the Mind of the Reader 15
Chapter 16: Teaching and the Flame Challenge 15
Chapter 17: Emotion Makes Memorable 16
Chapter 18: Story and the Brain 17
Chapter 19: Commonality 17
Chapter 20: Jargon and the Curse of Knowledge 18
Chapter 21: The Improvisation of Daily Life 18

KEY TAKEAWAYS **19**

Key Takeaway: Productive Listening Takes More than Just Your Ears.. *19*

Key Takeaway: Communication as a Group Experience 19

Key Takeaway: What's the Difference between Empathy and Theory of Mind *20*

Key Takeaway: Why Improv Creates Strong Groups *21*

Key Takeaway: Communication Goes beyond Words *21*

Key Takeaway: Reading Minds is the Key to Effective Communication.. *22*

Key Takeaway: Affective Empathy Improves Doctor-Patient Communication *23*

Key Takeaway: What Contributes to the Success of a Team *23*

Key Takeaway: Why Tuned-In Leadership Works *24*

Key Takeaway: Empathetic Strategy Differentiates Star Performers from Average Performers *25*

Key Takeaway: Affective Resonance and Effect of Empathy on Doctors *25*

Key Takeaway: Naming Emotions as a Way to Increase Empathy *26*

Key Takeaway: Explaining the Chemistry of Making Eye Contact.. *26*

Key Takeaway: Negative Use of Empathy *27*

Key Takeaway: All Readers Have Expectations *28*

Key Takeaway: Personal and Emotional Connection Turns Communication from Mundane to Memorable *29*

Key Takeaway: Transform Learning from a Dreary Experience to Memorable Experience *29*

Key Takeaway: How to Enhance Memory in a Presentation through Emotions *30*

Key Takeaway: The Brain Uses Stories to Organize Information in a Practical and Memorable Manner 30
Key Takeaway: Figuring out the Thoughts and Feelings of Others is Key in Communication 31
Key Takeaway: The Deception of Jargon 32
Key Takeaway: Effective and Flawless Communication Is Not a Formula 32

KEY LEARNING POINTS **34**

EDITORIAL REVIEW **36**

ABOUT THE AUTHOR **38**

EXECUTIVE SUMMARY

Who could be in a better place to show you the ropes of communication than a seasoned actor? With this kind of pedigree—and having spent several years working with scientists to help them communicate to an audience of lay people in reasonable and appreciated manner—Alan Alda puts down his knowledge on paper.

This book is a fantastic, albeit unusual, approach to the riddle of how to be effective in communication. It envisions excellent communication not just as a cleverness that can be acquired by learning steps or studying tips, but rather as a skill that only comes with a transformation of self.

The author begins by looking at the very core of good communication, relating with the audience. He elaborates on how to connect with an audience and explains some exercises to sharpen your ability such as mirror exercises and how to make communication clear and vivid.

In the second part, Alda takes you through what makes a person better at reading others. He explains the concept of empathy and the dark side of empathy. He touches on experiments that he subjected himself to due to constant inquisitiveness and the successes he obtained. Alda also elaborates on other important aspects of communication such as the importance of emotion, and use of jargon.

To wind up, Alda cuts down to the process of becoming an effective communicator. It's not just about successfully passing through steps, but rather learning from failure and using those failures to connect with others more profoundly in order to harness communication.

PART I: RELATING IS EVERYTHING

Chapter 1: Relating, It's the Cake

For a conversation to be productive, it's important for parties to listen and respond openly, but with sensitivity. Relating and active listening is what makes this possible. Relating is listening with your ears, eyes, and feelings. It is being aware of the other person's conduct such that everything about them informs your responses and probing. From their tone of voice to other subtle behaviors such as facial expressions or other "insignificant" activities such as their posture or position in the room.

Chapter 2: Theatre Games with Engineers

When dealing with professionals, communication often encounters the blockade of jargon. It's alright to use mumbo jumbo that's specific to your area of trade as long as the respondents know exactly what you mean. However, this is not always the case, even when dealing with people in the same profession. Also, several professionals think that they can be good communicators by merely listening or observing good communicators. However, this is not so. Good communication requires training and learning.

Chapter 3: The Heart and Head of Communication

Whenever we are communicating, we must try to be aware of what the other person is thinking and feeling. Similarly, if a person is to understand you, their heart and mind must work cohesively and resolve the back-and-forth between what is emotional and what is rational.

Authentic connection occurs when we can see people in a way that is both sound and emotional. To connect, you should understand the other person's feelings—or empathize—and have a consciousness of the other person's thoughts, also known as the Theory of the Mind.

Chapter 4: The Mirror Exercise

In the mirror exercise, two people, a leader and a follower, facing each other try to mimic a mirror. The leader has to act slowly enough to allow the 'follower' to connect and get in sync. It expresses the essence of communication. If you are communicating something, it's not merely the recipient's job to catch up, but it's the leader's responsibility to slow down and enable other people to follow. You can also practice the steps of mirroring with speech. Although more complicated, and has its fair share of skeptics, studies have shown that it works in building communication bridges.

Mirroring allows people to read each other's bodies and to pick up clues that help in reading emotions and thoughts.

Chapter 5: Observation Games

Synchrony only happens in an environment of careful observation. People see and respond to the slightest alteration in another person's behavior. Also, through observation, people express themselves and learn how to read other's behavior such as watching out for body language and tone of voice. This allows for communication to happen without necessarily using words.

By keenly observing other people's movements, body expressions, and tone of voice, people have a greater awareness of their own emotions because they see and sense what the other is feeling.

Chapter 6: Making it Clear and Vivid

Effective communication happens when the person communicating creates an effective story and understands what resonates and what doesn't resonate with the audience. You first have to make the audience want to know what you have to present. Then submit it concisely.

You must seek to make an emotional connection with the audience by expressing your presentation not just in ways you would find interesting, but also ways that other people find interesting in order to deepen their emotional connection.

Chapter 7: Reading Minds Helen Reiss and Matt Lerner

Most people share the opinion that empathy constitutes putting yourself in another's shoes and in some way relating to their emotions. However, if emotions momentarily swamp you, causing you to express empathy in an inappropriate way, it would be counterproductive.

When we pay more attention to subtle and involuntary gestures made by another person and respond accordingly, we receive more insight on their emotional state. It makes us more empathetic.

Chapter 8: Teams

What makes a great working team? Not the member's average intelligence level. According to Anita Woolley, a group's mean score on a standard empathy test was a more important contributor to the group's performance. Also, the ability of members to liberally participate, and the ratio of women in the group, are also significant factors. These findings apply to both physical and virtual groups. Entrepreneurs such as Jack Ma, the founder of Chinese e-commerce giant Alibaba, have known how to capitalize on some of these principles to aid the success of their companies.

Leadership is also a significant contributor to the success of a team. It's similar to the exercise of mirroring.

Chapter 9: Total Listening Starts with Where They Are

"Whereas leadership is critical, how leadership is communicated is just as important" (p. 12).

Typically, good communication begins with what is familiar to the audience and stops at a point where the audience still has an interest in what you have to say—otherwise they'll feel swamped.

When it comes to leadership, it matters how we relate with others. It's important that leaders express their thoughts plainly but keep in mind the audience's state of mind. A study by Golnaz Sadri found that it matters if managers show an understanding of people working under them.

Chapter 10: Listening from the Board Room to the Bedroom

Good communication is the responsibility of the individual delivering, not the recipient. When an audience doesn't understand the message, it is likely they will say no. The art of selling captures this model in the right way. Selling from the point of trying to address a customer's need has been proven to draw better results. Empathy helps us become more proactive and in control of other, seemingly involuntary, responses such as tone of voice or body language.

Chapter 11: Training Doctors to Have More Empathy

Dr. Helen Reiss had her eureka moment in communication when she willingly agreed to be vulnerable. It changed the way she related with her patients, and she had the urge to train other doctors. She first takes them through the neuroscience of empathy and informs doctors that they can learn to be more empathetic. After that, Helen coaches doctors on using the brain's ability to reflect what another person is experiencing. Lastly, she vouches for getting the patient's perspective which deepens the doctor-patient contact and enables the doctor to resonate emotionally with the patient—also known as having cognitive empathy. The patients receive not just treatment, but a life transforming experience.

PART II: GETTING BETTER AT READING OTHERS

Chapter 12: My Life as a Lab Rat

"Noting and attending to emotions improves one's ability to read other's emotions accurately."

Reading others is intriguing, but, can you improve your skills on empathy and Theory of Mind on your own? Alda thought it was possible and tried to exercise it by looking at other people and consciously attempting to describe the emotion they portray. The more active we are in studying the other person, the better we become at expressing empathy.

Chapter 13: Working Alone on Building Empathy

In a study that applied Baron Cohen's test of Reading the Mind in the Eyes, participants who went through meditation improved their ability to identify emotions as opposed to participants who went through regular lectures. By practicing meditation for a couple of minutes every day for several weeks, you can improve your ability to accurately decipher emotions from an eye gaze and be more empathetic. The eye gaze exercise releases a chemical known as Oxytocin which affects how much we trust and are willing to bond with other people.

Chapter 14: Dark Empathy

When we use our awareness of someone else's state of mind, not to sympathize but to beat them, this is the dark side of empathy. It is how interrogators know how to make prisoners feel helpless and weak. In the same way, charities or giant corporations use empathy to tip you from rational thinking into action. Empathy is not a cure for all, rather a tool that can work both ways, for good or bad.

Chapter 15: Reading the Mind of the Reader

It is possible to have a hunch of what's going on in the mind of an audience even when the audience is not with you in the room. For instance, when we write, whether an email, blog, or article we need to get to the point and keep it vivid, not get lost in detail.

To maintain the interest of a non-present audience, you ought to know their expectations and meet them. For instance, all readers expect thoughts to be laid out in a certain order. Being aware of a reader's expectations enables us to "read their minds." To achieve this, you have to take on another person's perspective.

Chapter 16: Teaching and the Flame Challenge

When teaching, there's a universal rule that says, "begin with what is known." However, knowing how to do it is an entirely different challenge. Whereas you could be providing valuable information, it can be quite soporific. The question begs, why teach something important when it isn't memorable?

To make a teaching more memorable, start with what is known. Then engage your audience by allowing some autonomy and room for discovery. Let the audience collaborate and build on ideas, establishing a personal connection with the class rather than just lecturing them.

Chapter 17: Emotion Makes Memorable

Emotional events like your first kiss or an embarrassing moment have a way of sticking in your head. We tend to remember events by linking them to strong emotions such as joy, disgust, and shame, among others. Amazingly, albeit awkwardly, body stress also enhances our memories and makes certain memories feel more important than others. Fear and laughter are some of the most powerful emotions that drive people to have clearer and more vivid memories of an event.

Emotions are not a prerequisite for remembrance, rather they strengthen our memory. Additionally, having more emotional content in any communication doesn't necessarily mean you'll get better or stronger memories.

Chapter 18: Story and the Brain

"Stories are a fundamental way through which the brain organizes information practically and memorably" (p. 11).

Many of us remember the opener from a famous soap opera, "Like sand through the hourglass, so are the days of our lives." Our days are full of stories. Stories are useful and are our greatest hope in introducing us to difficult concepts. Our brains are designed to use stories to understand, organize and store information in a memorable way.

Captivating stories have dramatic action; it makes the story more vivid and memorable. We can use stories to capture the imagination of an audience, impart wisdom to a child, or teach more difficult things such as arithmetic. Just remember, don't make it too easy for the leading character.

Chapter 19: Commonality

Storytelling is like the magic wand of communication. However, there's a crucial aspect of storytelling—if it's left out, it could end up making communication a bumpy road. Commonalities are vital in connecting with the audience. The more commonalities you have with the audience, the better the chance that they'll understand what you are communicating. This is why teachers seek to unearth what their students know so that they can build on that knowledge. The best communication occurs where we are not just alike, but where we are aware that we are alike.

Chapter 20: Jargon and the Curse of Knowledge

Jargon is a private language. It has an appealing aspect and can be intoxicating. Nearly all professions have developed their form of jargon. Although jargon hails from misty origins, it often has specific and useful meanings.

Using jargon to communicate to the right person can save time, tons of words, and help avoid errors. However, we must be careful when relating with people of different backgrounds because even words that seem simple to us can turn out to be indecipherable jargon.

Chapter 21: The Improvisation of Daily Life

In the process of Improv, there is no failure; each new step is a stride towards a satisfying resolution. As we move along, we connect and have a new perspective on things around us. When we pay attention to the fundamental reason behind a voice intonation, pacing, or facial expression we relate and respond to the audience like a leaf will sway in a gale.

KEY TAKEAWAYS

Key Takeaway: Productive Listening Takes More than Just Your Ears

When having a conversation, you could be listening with our ears, but your interaction could be impaired causing a disconnection with the other party. This often happens in the following circumstances:

• When we consciously or unconsciously focus on our assumptions concerning the topic of discussion rather than listen to the respondent.

• When we pay little or no attention to the other person's body language.

• When we ask questions that don't spring from the conversation.

To have an authentic dialogue and real communication, you need to be willing to listen openly, attentively, and naively. Ignorance backed-up with curiosity is an asset for genuine engagement. It brings out real humanity and develops a bond that releases humanness in our interactions.

Key Takeaway: Communication as a Group Experience

When working with groups, teams can go through different steps that build the ability to improvise to permeate the barriers of effective communication. The first step is to make the participants aware that the other person is a crucial partner in relating. The objective is to get the members not to ignore, but to acknowledge the actions of the other party. The next step is to develop and engage in activities that demand more talking and listening to another side. This way, even reserved and shy scientists can learn how to open up and expose their warm humanity, expressing themselves in new, more efficient ways.

Key Takeaway: What's the Difference between Empathy and Theory of Mind

Empathy is being able to discern another person's feelings even though they have not spoken about them. According to the theory of mirror neurons by Iacoboni, when we see human expressions that indicate pain or suffering in another person, mirror neurons within our brains help us viscerally feel the pain of the other person. Empathy helps us understand what's going on in the heart.

Theory of mind is being aware of what's going on in the other person's mind. We reflect on several experiences combined with keen attention on different forms of listening to develop an informed Theory of Mind. When we put together different expressions such as tone of voice, body language, facial expressions, and suggestive words, we can deduce what another person has in mind and thus communicate more efficiently.

Key Takeaway: Why Improv Creates Strong Groups

Synchrony is a pillar of Improv; it brings us together. Science has shown that synchronous marching strengthens cohesion and promotes cooperation among military personnel. The simple act of walking in step or tapping in sync produces greater collaboration and more trust. Simultaneous tapping gives members in a group a feeling of similarity and is more likely to have compassion for their tapping partners. Also, results from different studies indicate that synchronous tapping makes members in a group behave more altruistically towards each other.

When taken a notch higher, through leaderless mirroring, experienced improvisers display more rapid and more synchronized mirroring. Thus they are more in sync than when there is a leader.

Key Takeaway: Communication Goes beyond Words

In a team, people achieve synchrony when they observe each other's slightest body movements. They contribute individual efforts while aware they are part of a team, and therefore, cannot control the outcome by themselves. For instance, when handling imaginary glass tumblers, a person's body movements will differ from when he or she is handling an imaginary rubber ball. The coordination and drive to a specific objective of such an exercise in a team can happen even without a leader.

In a different scenario, a conversation can take place between two people without necessarily using plain words, but by expressing thoughts and observation. You can tell the relationship between two parties through interpreting expressions such as tone of voice, the way someone phrases statements, or even their body language.

Key Takeaway: Reading Minds is the Key to Effective Communication

Quite often, we think that reading minds is beyond our reach when it can be one of our most powerful tools in communication. The following steps can help you read the minds of your audience and in turn aid you to make your stories more vivid and clear.

First, assume the responsibility of making your audience develop an interest in your story, follow through, and understand what you are presenting. To achieve this, run through ideas that would make good entry points for your presentation and sustain it by making interesting points of discussion. Keenly observe the audience's movements, facial expressions, body language or body posture, and tone of voice and empathize.

By doing this, you'll develop a heightened awareness of what is in the mind of the audience and be better placed to establish an emotional connection by adding a human element to your presentation.

Key Takeaway: Affective Empathy Improves Doctor-Patient Communication

To improve on communication, doctors should appreciate that every person tends to read other people's minds. Just as a doctor would try to read the patient's facial expressions, body language or another indicator of emotions to diagnose a condition, patients also observe doctors to read their minds. Doctors can be trained to regulate their emotional response and avoid affective quick sand.

Matt Lerner accidentally learned that by adjusting the scenario to reflect life's unpredictability, kids in the autistic range become more interested and developed social skills and communication skills faster and better. Matt realized that by engaging autistic children in scenarios that were rather unlikely through exercises such as mirroring, and eventually acting out scenes from their daily lives, the children were more interested and could practice spontaneity which was more interesting to them.

Key Takeaway: What Contributes to the Success of a Team

Unlike for an individual where their IQ level is a good predictor of how the person will perform various tasks, teams rely on other factors. In a study of the key factors of what drives performance in both physical and virtual groups, some teams worked better and had superior achievements as compared to others. The successful teams had members who communicated a lot, participated equally, and possessed excellent emotional reading skills. High scores in empathy are a product of good emotional reading skills. Here, women score better than men. Women are more liberal in expressing themselves and have higher levels of participation which hinge on Improv's most essential element: listening and listening now.

Key Takeaway: Why Tuned-In Leadership Works

Several studies have shown that tuned-in leadership gives better results than tough leadership. Tools of Improv can explain this notion. When a leader admonishes a member or the entire team, he or she can choose to point out the error and give a stern warning. Alternatively, the leader can reflect on what is genuinely working out well for the team and urge them to bring their "game" up to the same level. This is using the Improv principle of Yes And. It's not just about softening the blow; it's keeping in mind the other person's thoughts and emotions. Tuned leadership through keen listening gives leaders a better perspective when onboarding as opposed to realizing you've had the wrong candidate much later. Within the first couple of minutes of an onboarding conversation, through total listening, a leader can know who the candidate is, what they can offer, and discern what they can expect from them.

Key Takeaway: Empathetic Strategy Differentiates Star Performers from Average Performers

Star performers stand out because they are more emotionally aware of their prospects and empathize. They can identify a prospective client's needs and match them to the right products or services. As described by Daniel Goleman, they use social awareness. They become aware of the target's primal inner state (empathize), then grasp their feelings and thoughts (theory of mind and thought), and finally get "complicated" social solutions.

Empathy also enables someone to be more patient. This is why star sales performers can target a long-term relationship that eventually has a bigger pay out as compared to short-term associations.

Key Takeaway: Affective Resonance and Effect of Empathy on Doctors

Affective resonance is the feeling of connectedness we can get with other people. For instance, when you look someone in the eye or when our bodies are falling into synch with another person's. These mirror functions happen almost automatically. When we tune into someone else, in a way, it creates a sensation of sharing an emotion. Affective resonance is an avenue that can cultivate empathy. Doctors who practice greater empathy get better results with their patients. Expressing empathy and interest, supplying information on a condition and its treatment makes a significant difference in the patients. The patients are more likely to follow through on such a doctor's recommendations. Also, showing empathy reduces the possibility of malpractice suits appreciably.

Key Takeaway: Naming Emotions as a Way to Increase Empathy

Naming emotions involves focusing on what the other person seems to be feeling and then identifying the feeling. It is related to therapeutic alliance: the bond between a therapist and a client. This is when a customer identifies what he or she is feeling and says it to their therapist. In building the bond, the therapist recognizes what matters in the emotion and responds accordingly with statements like, "That must be painful for you." Being aware of the other person's emotional state can help you be less judgmental, more patient, and more confident. By identifying the other person's emotion, it does not make you more sympathetic. Rather, it helps you respond more appropriately.

Key Takeaway: Explaining the Chemistry of Making Eye Contact

Baron Cohen's test of Reading the Mind in the Eyes is a great self-instructing approach to improving levels of empathy. It involves looking at another person's eyes only and correctly identifying the emotions. The test is available on the internet for anyone willing to have a go.

The eye gaze affects brain chemistry and is critical to communication. It causes the release of Oxytocin, a chemical in the brain which influences how much we trust other people and bond with them. Popularly referred to as the love hormone, studies have shown that Oxytocin is released when there is eye contact even between individuals and pets they love. Making eye contact is a great way for improving empathy. However, several suggestions exist on how to increase your empathy levels. For example, the magazine *Psychology Today* recommends watching TV on low volume and practicing non-verbal interpretation of the relationships between the characters and what they are discussing.

Key Takeaway: Negative Use of Empathy

A U.S. Congress report written in 2005 recorded the details of how pharmaceutical giant Merck and Company sold their products unethically. Although the company had already frozen new sales of a leading drug, Viox, due to its adverse effects, company reps were on instruction not to discuss its dark side thus not stopping subsequent sales. On the contrary, the company trained their sales teams how to use verbal and nonverbal techniques to win over a target physician and get him or her to trust them more. They learned how to give long handshakes and how to dine. They were taught how to move their eyes, heads, fingers and even legs and subtly communicate using body posture, facial expression and mirroring.

The company's training manual described mirroring as a way to match patterns with intent to enter into the customer's world. It trains them to subconsciously raise the level of trust by building bridges of similarity. This was great advice for closing a deal, but not so good when you knew the deal would eventually harm the other party.

Key Takeaway: All Readers Have Expectations

Without the benefit of being able to see their audience or observe their body language, facial expressions or tone of voice, writers seem to have an uphill task of communicating. However, George Gopen, a Professor Emeritus of Rhetoric at Duke University reckons that all readers have expectations. He believes that each reader has basic expectations which the writer has to meet, otherwise they will frustrate and lose the reader.

According to George, the expectations are:

• Each reader expects thoughts to be laid out in a certain order.

• Each reader expects to hear what the sentence is about at the beginning, not in the middle.

• Readers anticipate that a sentence will be a tale about whoever appears first. A verb should follow soon after outlining the main character.

• Each reader expects that what comes at the end of a sentence has particular importance. He describes it as the stress position.

Key Takeaway: Personal and Emotional Connection Turns Communication from Mundane to Memorable

Establishing a personal connection with an audience is a two-way street. Sometimes it requires us to expose something personal and be willing to be seen by the audience for you to see them. It engages the audience intimately and opens doors to connect to their emotions.

Descriptions are sometimes best made using emotional terms. However, they have to be crafted in an appropriate way and for the right audience. This way, you can transform a seemingly mundane presentation into a truly memorable one

Key Takeaway: Transform Learning from a Dreary Experience to Memorable Experience

The first principle of teaching is that you should start with what is familiar with them. Then allow the learners the joy of discovery by giving them some autonomy. Both these approaches involve empathy and Theory of Mind. Recognition of what the audience already knows and what they want to know. For example, instead of repeatedly lecturing groups of students on different concepts, a more efficient way to communicate would be to engage them with intriguing puzzles and have the students come up with arguments and solutions. As the students collaborate and have fun, they absorb necessary information. Personal and emotional connections structured in an appropriate way to the right audience will deliver the punch and make presentations or teaching more memorable.

Key Takeaway: How to Enhance Memory in a Presentation through Emotions

If you want an audience to have a clearer memory of anything you communicate, it is best when you link the performance with emotion. However, the kind of emotion matters. For example, laughter, which is one of the most powerful and memory grinding emotions, is not just good for making the memory stick, it's also a good way to connect and spur engagement. Fear is also a powerful and easy to recall emotion that makes events or presentations more memorable.

But how do you deliver it to an audience?

One of the best ways to stir emotions in an audience and get them to remember what you are presenting is by sharing short, moving, and (where possible) personal stories. Audiences are often captivated by and relish short stories. As they connect with the emotion, you can pass on a point or two of what you want to communicate more powerfully and memorably.

Key Takeaway: The Brain Uses Stories to Organize Information in a Practical and Memorable Manner

When a person whose left and right hemispheres of the brain operate independently (an individual whose corpus callosum is disconnected) makes a strange choice, the interpreter side of the brain comes up with a plausible explanation. This happens even though the interpreter hemisphere, the left side, has no clue of what is going on. It would figure out, quibble, justify and search for a cause and effect to give a reasonable answer.

When you tell a story, our brains get coupled fascinatingly. If you are watching a movie when plugged into an fMRI machine, the parts of your brain that are active will also activate when telling the story of the film. Even more impressive is that when another group of people listens to a recording of your narration, the same activity patterns will show in their brains. It's like they watched the same movie.

Key Takeaway: Figuring out the Thoughts and Feelings of Others is Key in Communication

Learning is a social process and interaction. The relationship between the learner and students forms its basis. For teachers to be more efficient, they must figure out, as much as possible, the thought process of their students to understand the cause of where they make mistakes. With more familiarity, a sense of similarity positively influences communication and positively impacts learning.

Familiarity helps us to sync up with one another. When we remind an audience of our common areas, they become more receptive to our communication and may accept it. It could make an otherwise tense conversation more civil and productive. Familiarity is what draws us to watch sequels of movies even though we suspect they may not be as catchy. It makes an audience more receptive to our communication and perhaps even accept it.

Key Takeaway: The Deception of Jargon

People often use jargon to make to make them look and sound smarter. The irony is, if the recipient gets what you are communicating, then it means he or she is equally smart or even smarter. On the other hand, if the recipient doesn't understand the jargon, you don't get your message across, and the content of your communication doesn't sound all that smart when it's incomprehensible.

Jargon hides the very thing that you want to communicate, and we are so quickly pulled into its deception. According to you, it is an amazing expression of what you'd like to put across. But we are often oblivious to the fact that the recipient might not have a clue as to what we are discussing. The more knowledge we have, the more we can't imagine what it's like not to have that knowledge. This way having additional knowledge becomes a burden, a hindrance to effective communication because we cannot take the beginners point of view.

Key Takeaway: Effective and Flawless Communication Is Not a Formula

Communication is like a dance between the presenter and the audience, the author, and the reader. They move together making graceful moves and taking joy in every step of the tango. Every effort we make to find a means which the recipient will have a better perspective is a positive step towards being in sync and dancing with your partner, the recipient.

A list of tips or a formula will not result in good communication. It calls for a wholesome transformation of self. It requires regular practicing of behaviors such as making contact with other people, deepening connections with responses of Yes And., and paying attention to the fundamental source of indirect communication.

KEY LEARNING POINTS

• What is relating? It is being so aware of the other person that even when you have turned your back on them, you are observing them. It's letting everything about them affect you, not just their words but also their tone of voice, body language or even positioning in the room.

• When we see someone else suffering or going through pain, mirror neurons help us to read his or her facial expressions and make us viscerally feel the other person's pain.

• We all naturally possess strengths that make empathy and Theory of Mind possible. However, we rarely call them into play

• The average intelligence of a group is not a significant predictor of a group's performance. Rather the ability of members to freely participate in discussions and the member's average score on standardized tests for empathy are.

• The three rules of three: Try and make no more than three points; Explain difficult concepts in three different ways; make an important point three times.

• Even if we presume that empathy is a tool for good we should always remember that there are people who will try use it for their selfish gain.

• Being aware of a reader's expectations gives us a glimpse of what the reader will be going through.

• Sometimes, being willing to see the other person means you have to be willing to have them see you.

- When Doctors learn to express greater empathy, not only do they get higher empathy scores but their patients get better.

EDITORIAL REVIEW

If I Understood You, Would I Have This Look on My Face? By Alan Alda is an interesting compilation of various experiences by the author on the science and art of communicating. The book is an attempt to educate the reader on a behavioral change that would bring about more efficient communication. The author uses several personal experiences, stories, and results from scientific studies to illustrate how people succeed or fail in executing good communication. Alda also shares several personal experiences to paint vivid pictures of different concepts of communication.

While it is commendable to use anecdotes to drive a point home, the reader may find it difficult to keep track of the main idea being discussed, or get lost in the jungle of stories. The sheer number of personal narratives and repetition of key aspects, such as empathy can confuse readers.

Despite this, the book is a good contribution to the art and science of communication overall. It is reasonably written, but it fails to model what it seeks to preach: effective communication. The book bears a long title that barely illuminates its contents. Also, the author asserts that the responsibility of ensuring effective communication lies entirely with the giver of the message, which is not quite accurate. A reader or listener has the responsibility to pay attention and avoid distractions.

Emphasis on the leader role takes center stage in the book's sections. The first part lays prominence on the importance of relating. Alan elaborates on how connecting to the audience is fundamental in the communication process. He uses his experiences with the mirror exercises and observation games to demonstrate leader and follower roles in communication.

Section two focuses on improving the skills of reading others. Here, Alan discusses pertinent issues in the development of this ability such as developing an inkling of what is in the mind of an audience, empathy, commonality and a description of how the brain uses stories to store information logically and recall more vividly. Like the first section, this part is also jam-packed with narrations of Alan's personal experiences and exploits. The second part deeply explores empathy and closes with a call to the reader to seek not just knowledge and tips for good communication, but a transformation of self.

ABOUT THE AUTHOR

Alan Alda is a seasoned award-winning actor and film writer both in Hollywood and in Broadway. His love for science drew him to host *Scientific American Frontier* a scientific talk show on PBS for 11 years. He has won several awards for outstanding work in communicating science and is a visiting professor at Stony Brook University, Alan Alda Center for Communicating Science. He's married to Arlene and loves to hang out with his grandchildren.

THE END

If you enjoyed this summary, please leave an honest review on Amazon.com…it'd mean a lot to us.

If you haven't already, we encourage you to purchase a copy of the original book.

Made in the USA
San Bernardino, CA
09 August 2017